the LETTER BLUES

By Anne Meeker Watson
Illustrated by Stacey Lamb

To my daddy, who loved letters, words and books as much as I do – Anne

To the Lamb Fam, the Leslie Clan and the Fischer Gang – Stacey

This is the B sound.
Lips go BOP!
Buh, buh, buh, buh, buh, buh, BUH.

This is the P sound.
Lips go POP!
Puh, puh, puh, puh, puh, puh, PUH.

Buh, buh, buh, BUH.
Puh, puh, puh, PUH.

You can sing the Letter Blues!

Do the
*Head
Dance.*

This is the H sound.
Hand is hot!
Huh, huh, huh, huh, huh, huh, HUH.

This is the M sound.
Hum a lot.
Mmmmmmmmmm.

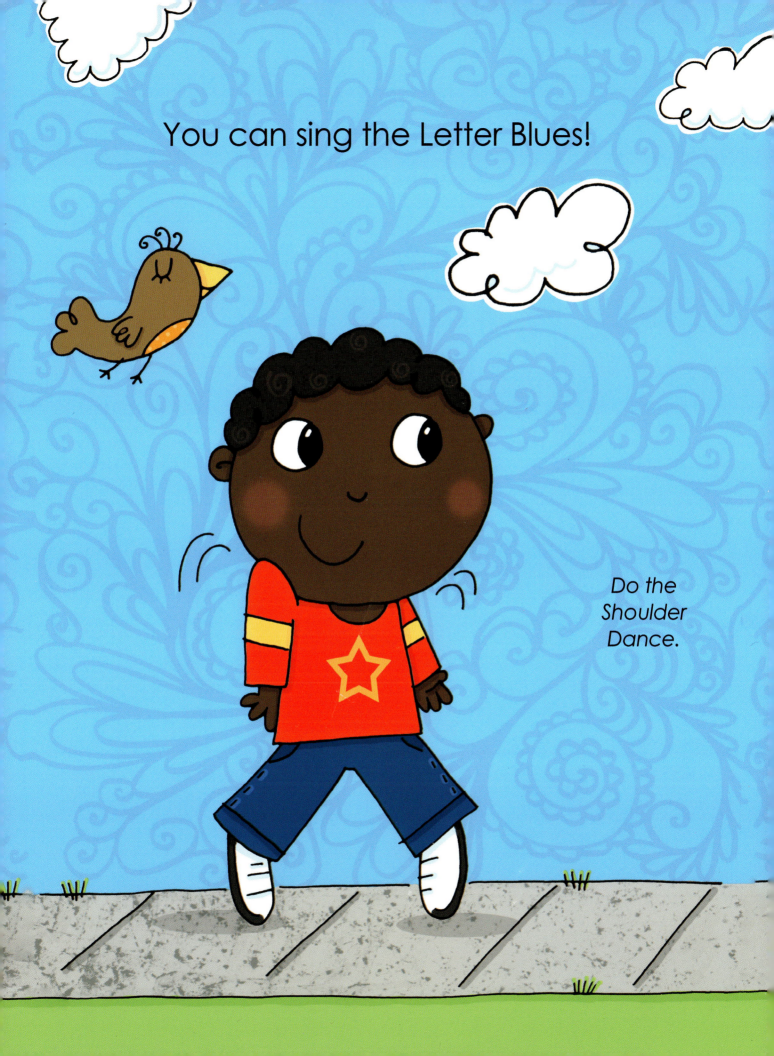

This is the S sound.
Make it long!
Ssssssssssssssss.

This is the W.
Make it strong!
Wuh, wuh, wuh, wuh, wuh, wuh, WUH.

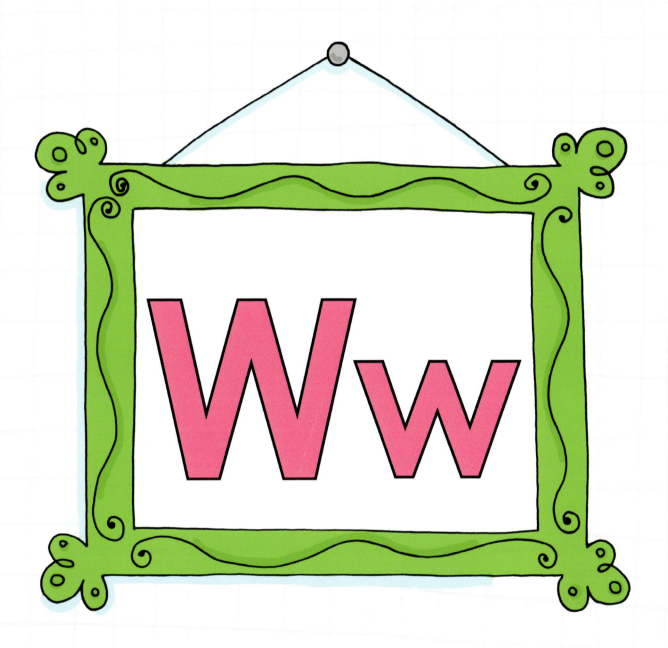

You can sing the Letter Blues!

Do the
Knee
Dance.

Letter sounds are fun to sing.

They make your tongue feel crazy.

Letters make the words we say,
like **ladybug** and **daisy**.

ladybug

daisy

Buh, buh, buh, buh, buh, buh, BUH.
bouncy ball

b • • • • •

Puh, puh, puh, puh, puh, puh, PUH.

puppy dog

p • • • • • •

Huh, huh, huh, huh, huh, huh, HUH.

helicopter

h

Mmmmmmmmmmmm.
maracas

m • • • • •

Sssssssssssss.

sea gull

s • • • • •

Wuh, wuh, wuh, wuh, wuh, wuh, WUH.
wagon ride

w • • • • •

Letter Knowledge
Activities to help young children learn and grow

Learning to read, for the brain, is a lot like an amateur ringmaster first learning how to organize a three-ring circus. He wants to begin individually and then synchronize all the performances. It only happens after all the separate acts are learned and practiced long and well.

-Maryanne Wolf

Alphabet learning actually begins from birth. When parents read aloud to their children from the start, they are exposing them to letters and language within the context of colorful and engaging books. Children who consistently enjoy the intimacy of reading with a caring adult learn to love stories. They understand that books contain print, and that print is made up of letters.

There are fun ways to teach individual letters for every age. Babies love sound play and enjoy imitating letter sounds. Add a gentle bounce or rock as you say or sing "buh-buh-buh-BABY!" or "duh-duh-duh-DADDY!" Toddlers enjoy colorful picture books with objects they can label by pointing to them on the page. The focus for toddlers is on increasing their vocabulary and exposing them to print in books. Preschoolers might like to trace large letters in print with their finger or a marker. Introduce her to the letters of her name and provide ample praise for any letters she can recall.

There is no evidence that early interest in letters is related to more advanced reading skills, so include letter learning only if your child is interested. Give her playful opportunities to recognize the shapes and sounds of letters, talk about the letters in all of the favorite things in her world, and "write" with scribbles, lines, circles and shapes. As she grows, she will eventually identify letters by sight and sound, and trace and copy letters.

Here are some practical tips for teaching your child to identify letters by sight and sound.

MOVE YOUR BODY

Pool Pointers. Pool noodles are fun and colorful, and children love them. Cut one in half and use it as a silly pointer for your child to practice his letter sounds. Print one letter on a single sheet of paper. Repeat this task for a total of three to five letters and place them on the floor. Tell your child to point to the letter of his choice and make its sound. Chant the letter sound with him as he taps the printed letter and says "puh-puh-puh" for the letter P or "huh-huh-huh" for the letter H.

Letter Tag. Children love to run! Make racing into letter fun by playing an alphabet tag game. Print one letter on a single sheet of paper. Repeat this task for a total of three to five letters and place them on the floor or tape them to the wall. Instruct your players to line up at the starting line. Tell them to run to the letters, touch the letter 'T,' then run back to finish the game. Repeat for a different letter.

LET'S PLAY AND PRETEND

ABC Racecars. Young children love to play with miniature cars and racecar tracks. Add a sticker or tape a piece of paper with a letter name on top of a handful of racecars. Show your child how to describe the actions of the cars by using their alphabet names. For instance, "A" may be the fastest car, or "G" may crash coming around the curve.

Label the Play in My Day. An awareness that printed words have meaning is an important pre-literacy skill for youngsters, and a prerequisite to letter learning. Organize your child's play area as you pair print awareness with his favorite toys. Simply print the name of each play item on a piece of paper and tape the label to the appropriate toy container. Point to the labels as you ask your child what he would like to play: BLOCKS or PUZZLE? You can add a photo of the toy next to the printed label if the storage boxes for each are identical. Printed labels also help children learn to put toys away independently. Your child will feel proud that she can "read" her toy containers and tell you that BLOCKS starts with 'B!'

LOVING OTHERS...AND MYSELF!

Letter Touch Time. Most young children crave time spent in your lap cuddling, reading and sharing moments with you. Include a game of letter learning by drawing a letter with your pointer on your child's palm. Take turns so that your child draws letters on your palm as well. What letter did you draw? This lovely and simple activity connects your child's sense of touch with his thinking skills. You can also draw letters with your pointer on your child's back as he transitions to nap or bedtime or craves quiet and connection with you. Continue the game until your child decides to stop – or falls sound asleep.

Name that Tune. Make up a song that includes her name and letters. For instance, you could sing: "Your name is Katie, K-A-T-I-E!" You can add to your child's special song by including a compliment for her, or a description of her favorite activity or toy. If you don't feel comfortable composing your own melody, borrow a familiar tune, such as "Mary Had a Little Lamb" or "Twinkle, Twinkle Little Star." Your child will love her special song when you sing it with her and will memorize the letters of her song quickly and easily.

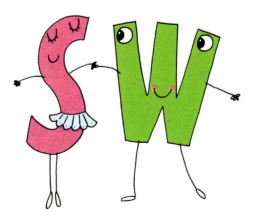

GET READY TO READ

Personalized Placemats. Purchase a package of 11 x 17-inch construction paper, stickers and washable markers. Invite your child to the kitchen to help you prepare for a meal. His job is to make a placemat for each person who will eat with him at the kitchen table. Your child can write the first letter of each name by tracing the pattern you draw for him or copying an example you draw on the placemat. He can add stickers to ornament his handwriting. Each placemat is a special gift to the person joining you for a meal, and a personalized message from your child to its recipient.

Up or Down, Sight or Sound? Should children learn upper- or lowercase letters first? And is it best to start by teaching letter sounds, or should children first memorize letters by sight? The answer is: teach it all! Children will read books with you that have both lower- and uppercase letters, so identify both for her. Play games that match lower- and uppercase letters and teach her how to recognize and write her name using both upper- and lowercase letters. Children also have different learning preferences. Some children learn best when instruction is presented visually, and others learn best by listening. Teach the ABCs by sharing visual examples of the letters AND play with the sounds each letter makes. This comprehensive approach will make letter learning fun and interesting for your child.

MORE BOOKS TO READ

Check out these wonderful alphabet books:

A is for Angry: An Animal and Adjective Alphabet by Sandra Boynton
A was Once an Apple Pie by Edward Lear
Dr. Seuss's ABC: An Amazing Alphabet by Dr. Seuss
Chicka Chicka Boom Boom by Bill Martin Jr. and John Archambault
Eric Carle's ABC by Eric Carle
Old Black Fly by Jim Aylesworth

ABOUT THIS ACTIVITY GUIDE

The goal of the activity guide is to share activities that you can enjoy with the children you love while connecting with them in a more meaningful way. Music combined with play, rich picture book literature and YOU as a child's play partner create the engagement a young child needs to learn and grow. My SING.PLAY.LOVE.® songs, books, movies and activities can be powerful tools for supporting the development—and delight—of your youngster.

The Letter Blues

Swing

1. This is the B sound, lips go BOP!   B-b-b-b-b-b-b!
2. This is the H sound, hand is hot.   H-h-h-h-h-h-h!
3. This is the S sound, make it long.   S-s-s-s-s-s-s!

This is the P sound lips go POP!   P-p-p-p-p-p-p!
This is the M sound, hum a lot.   M-m-m-m-m-m-m!
This is the "Double - you," make it strong.   W-w-w-w-w-w-w!

B-b-b-b!   P-p-p-p!   You can sing the Let-ter Blues!
H-h-h-h!   M-m-m-m!
S-s-s-s!   W-w-w-w!

Let-ter sounds are fun to sing. They make your tongue feel cra-zy.__

Let-ters make the words we say__ like "la-dy bug" and "daisy!"__

B-b-b-b-b-b-b!   *(Spoken) Bouncy Ball!*

P ... p ... p ... p ... p ... p ... p ... Puppy Dog
H ... h ... h ... h ... h ... h ... h ... Helicopter
Mmmmmmmmmmmmmmm ... Maracha
Sssssssssssssssssssssssssssssssssss ... Seagull
W ... w ... w ... w ... w ... w ... w ... Wagon ride

Anne loves letters, words and books. Her idea of a perfect day is to sit on her front porch and read an entire novel in one sitting (with a bag of Dove dark chocolates). Anne's friend Allison came up with the idea for this song and waited patiently for Anne to get busy composing it.

Anne Meeker Watson, Ph.D., MT-BC is a singer/songwriter, music therapist and teacher of little children, as well as grown-ups who work in early childhood education. Her job is to make cool stuff to share with kids and their caring adults.

Stacey Lamb is an artist but likes to think of herself more as a Master Doodler and a Professional Dreamer. She has two children, Emily and Scott. She and her husband live in the country with lots of owls, possums, coyotes, wild turkeys and bugs. Stacey loves illustrating and writing stories that make kids feel warm inside. She cannot imagine doing anything better, except perhaps working in an ice cream factory! Check out Stacey and her fun products at *www.thisishappytown.com*.

SING.PLAY.LOVE.® educational products – including songs, music videos, picture books and other resources – are fun and engaging for both children and their caring adults. When used in combination, SING.PLAY.LOVE.® products provide the repetition and enrichment young children need to practice new skills and prepare for kindergarten success.

Visit **SingPlayLove.com** for more fun products to support early learning, kindergarten readiness and FUN.

Library of Congress Control Number: 2016911802

ISBN: 978-1-945598-53-1

SING.PLAY.LOVE.® BOOKS published by Meeker Creative LLC, Kansas City, Missouri.

SingPlayLove.com